Membership Sit
Educating with WordPress

by

Scott A. Gardner

Other books by Scott A. Gardner:

Recognized Expert Status

Published by Dark Raptor Press
PO Box 2242
Clay, NY 13041
www. DarkRaptor.com
sales@darkraptor.com

First print version September 2014

My thanks and appreciation to all the clients who have asked me to help them set up membership sites. We've learned a lot together!

Table of Contents

Introduction

Let me start off by saying this is not a book on "how to make millions in passive income." It's not about making money at all, since some membership sites don't charge for access. No, this book is about **designing** a membership site. This is about the nuts-and-bolts of how a membership site is put together. This is the book I wanted to find when I started putting together membership sites, but couldn't. So after a lot of trial and error, and asking stupid questions of a lot of people, I sat down and wrote the book I was looking for.

That's not to say it's about membership site software. It's true I discuss several software programs here, but the book is mostly software independent. I'll be talking about using WordPress as a base on which to build your site, but there are several other options. I use WordPress as the basis for several membership sites myself, including the companion site for the book – www.MembershipSiteMoney.com. (Don't worry – this book isn't one big advertisement for my site!) But you could use almost any platform and follow the outline here, and you should come up with a decent site.

I'll be outlining a process that will give you a fully functional membership site. But it will also be one that's simple to use as a member, and also simple to administer. Unless you recruit someone else, you're likely to be the administrator, so you should appreciate that part!

There are many reasons to start a membership site and a lot of different types of content to fill them with. I'm mainly going to be focusing on teaching sites; that is sites where the content is intended to transfer a set of information to each member. If you want to build what I call a clubhouse site – one where members come and interact for recreational purposes - you can apply the same process to building one of those too.

Some sites are simple; you're either a member or you aren't. Some are more complex and involve information segments or levels, with different content for each. Some sites award badges (little pictures that the members can display) for completing the course content. Some sites have multiple levels of prices depending on which level you join, and others are completely free. But all of these types of sites can be built using the concepts outlined here.

We're going to start at the beginning, making no assumptions about how much you know about membership sites. Feel free to skip chapters and focus on the information you need. Read the book, and at the end is an Action Items list you can use to create your own membership site. There's no test, so enjoy!

I wish you health, happiness and prosperity!

Scott A. Gardner

Why WordPress?

WordPress was created as blogging software – a sort of on-line journal. And it still functions wonderfully as such! But WordPress can also be used as a Content Management System (CMS), allowing someone who knows nothing about coding or working with web sites to actually run one.

There are two versions of WordPress. The first one, located at WordPress.com, allows you to set up a blog on their site for free and run it. The address will be something like "MyFantasticBlog.WordPress.com." You can give this address out freely and visitors can come here and read your profound words of wisdom.

The other site, WordPress.org, allows you to download the software and install it – again at no charge – to your own web site. You can customize your WordPress installation with all sorts of add-ons.

Many people choose WordPress to build their site around because it is free, and relatively easy to figure out. There are thousands of WordPress sites installed around the world, in dozens of languages, and thousands of certified and non-certified experts who can help you do almost anything with it.

The software itself is fairly plain. It allows you to create pages, and set up one specific page for showing your blog posts. But it has many "hooks," or places that developers can add in software that does specific jobs. Membership software is one such type of plug-in. You can also get your site translated into other languages, add in calendars where visitors can schedule their own appointments with you, add in discussion boards. . . Literally almost any modification you can think of is already out there, in probably a dozen different versions.

Your posts, which are probably where a lot of your membership content will be stored, are meant to be text based. But you can also add audio or video content to them and attach files for display or download. You can give your members a true multi-media learning experience quite easily.

For the purposes of this book, we're going to suggest that you register your own domain name and install the latest version of WordPress to the root directory. Registering a domain name will probably cost you about $15 per year. Web hosting space can range from $5/month to several hundred dollars per year, depending on how robust the host is, and how much help and what types of services they offer.

We're not going to offer a walk-though for WordPress installation and administration here. Please check the *Links* chapter near the back of the book for help with this and other instructions that are beyond the scope of this book. No worries – we've hooked you up!

Uses of a Membership Site

A membership site can be used for almost any reason imaginable. There are as many different types of membership sites as there are reasons for joining one. This book focuses on creating educational or learning sites; sites that consist mainly of content behind a membership "wall" that are meant to teach the members new or interesting information, concepts or knowledge.

This specialized information can be lumped together, or broken up into segments or levels (courses). Simple sites will allow the member to access all the information at once and trust them to work through it in order, at their own speed. A more complex site can be set up to "drip" the contents to a user at given intervals, like a given number of days apart, or when they've indicated that they finished one lesson and are ready to move on to the next one.

The main purpose of membership software is to provide a wall keeping general site visitors out, while allowing recognized individuals – members – to access restricted content. Again, this book is about sites that teach, but the restricted content could be a collection of digital content, or even just an areas where people with a shared interest can chat back and forth. If you think about it, music streaming sites like Spotify and Pandora are just huge membership sites with a customized way of accessing the restricted content.

One of the best reasons for having a membership site is to keep a list or database of all the members and their contact information. You can track who is seeing the restricted content and keep in touch with them to let them know about revised content, new lessons, and so forth. Verified contacts, especially ones that have proven they want your information, are an important sales resource.

Here are just a few of the types of membership sites that you might set up:

- Coaching or consulting

- Digital collection access

- Clubhouse

- Social or political groups

- Specialized education

- Collaborative work

- *And many, many more!*

We're not going to tell you what type of site to set up and you certainly don't have to stop with just one. Feel free to experiment. The information in this book can help you with almost any type of restricted access site you want to set up.

As you begin to design your site, you will want to keep the end in mind. What do you want each user to do once they've completed a course? Perhaps you have higher levels of information they can access at the same site. Perhaps you want to move them into a more intensive and costly program or perhaps you simply want to let them hang around for as long as they like. Any of these options are fine. After all, it's your site. With learning sites, we find that these are perfect vehicles for moving members into other programs. Just be ready to design an ending for your members, as needed.

Before You Begin

There are a number of questions you should ask yourself as you begin to jot your design ideas down. The very first one is: Should I be using a membership site at all? There are options for simpler systems, like putting your content in a password protected directory and giving out the one password to all who want to access that information. I have a client who does that with the presentations from their annual conference.

If you're putting together a number of courses, or you want several courses created and taught by different instructors, a more robust teaching platform, like Moodle, might be appropriate. It's designed to offer different types of content, administer quizzes, and produce number or letter grades for each student upon completion of a course.

Another consideration is time. Do you want to start a bunch of students at the same time, or can a student start whenever they want? Can they access all course materials at once and complete it at their own pace, or will you drip content out at certain intervals?

What do you want to teach? If this knowledge is something only you know, then you're stuck having to come up with the course contents on your own. Maybe you've already written a book or series of articles. Maybe you created a video program. You can re-craft the information into different lessons, different courses. Or you may pull information from other sources, other authors or creators. A text file from one person, an audio interview with another one.

You also need a target market. This is the group of people to whom you want to advertise your membership site, people who might be interested in joining. If you know the type of content you want to offer, this should give you a good idea of the target market. Advanced skateboarding lessons aren't likely a good fit for most senior financial analysts, while most tween girls aren't interested in a course about applying horror movie special effects make-up.

You should begin making a list of the general and specific content you want on the site and how you're going to structure it, by lessons and by courses. How will this content be presented? Will it be text-based? On-line only? Or will you allow members to download files like PDFs and audio or video files? Do you have all the hardware and software you need to generate this content and to make it available to your members?

Do you have the time and experience to administer all the lessons, courses and levels on your own? If not, you can either recruit or hire one or more people to help you. I help run a (non-membership) WordPress-based restaurant review site that has several people logging in to write reviews, a couple editors who can proofread the text reviewers leave and two administrators who can push the button to publish the content on the site.

You also need to decide if you will charge for access to the membership area. I know there are several dozen books out there claiming you can make a million dollars with a membership site while sitting back and doing nothing. This is not one of those books! However, you can charge for access and make some coin if you successfully reach the correct target market. You can have a mix of membership levels; the first level may give some general information for free (in exchange for valid contact information, which can be worth more than what you'd charge for access to the information), and the higher levels give more specialized information in exchange for payment.

As far as taking payment, there are many credit card processors out there you can sign up with. Many charge a percentage of each transaction plus a small set fee per transaction. Some even levy a monthly charge to process your payments. Then there are others like PayPal and Stripe that charge you per transaction and that's it. Even Amazon has opened its own on-line payment service. [NOTE: not all membership site software programs hook into all payment processors. You'll need to check with each one and see if it can handle your processor of choice.]

A basic WordPress installation, plus some basic text-based content, should take up less than 100 MB of space on your host's server. However, unless you know you won't be taking up that much space, I'd recommend going with at least 250 MB of space. This gives your site room to grow and to store lesson content. I ***do not*** recommend going with a host who offers you "unlimited space." Remember, they're offering that to each and every one of their other customers too and some of them are going to take as much space as possible. More importantly, they will also take the computing power of that server, leaving you with a slow-running site.

If you're going to be serving video content as part of your lessons, space and speed are additional considerations. I would, however, suggest you store your videos on another site instead. Having some content on YouTube is great, but then everyone has access to that, registered member of your site or not. I'd put certain videos, like the welcome video for your free section on YouTube where it will be indexed and reported on Google and other search engines, where people can trip over it and find you. There are cloud services like Amazon's S3 service, or Google Cloud, where you can store your videos, and Vimeo has semi-pro and professional options as well. I'd investigate those and choose the one best suited to your needs.

Each page on your site, and every post, has the option for readers to comment. Many membership plug-ins either restrict this automatically, or offer you the option of doing this on each post and page. If you want to interact with your members, or if you want them to interact with one another, letting them comment on each post or lesson is the simplest option. However, if you want to foster deeper discussions, and offer them more options for commenting – or just to natter back and forth – installing a forum plug-in might be the way to go. These require some additional setup on installation, and they're another thing you or someone else is going to need to administer. However, for certain types of sites they can be invaluable.

Many sites now offer badges to members. A badge is simply a small picture that shows the user has finished some task. The Open Badges project web site is probably the best place to learn all about these. You can install a plug-in that awards badges to users upon completion of a lesson, course or level. Badges are still relatively new out there, and changes are taking place rapidly. If they're something you want to offer your members, it's best to stay up on the current discussions about them, and keep your software updated.

Speaking of finishing, you should have a plan for how you want the course or level to end. Maybe it's a lesson that ties together all the other information you've presented. Perhaps it's an interactive lesson where they show off what they've learned. Maybe it's just a simple message of congratulations, or the awarding of a certificate or license. Maybe you have higher levels you want them to move to – that's how many of the sites I set up end most levels or courses. Whatever it is, you should begin planning for it now, and figure out how you want to present this to your members.

Once you've answered all of these concerns for yourself, you'll be about 80% done with the planning process.

What You'll Need

This chapter is going to present you with a list of all the things you'll need to have a successful educational membership site. Some of the items you'll pull together from the 'net, and others you'll have to create yourself (or have others create them for you). If you see one or more items listed that you don't understand yet, don't worry, there's still quite a bit of information coming in the following chapters.

• A registered website name (URL)

• Website host with enough space

• Membership site plug-in

• Payment processor (if collecting money)

• External mailing list management account

- Aweber

- MailChimp

- Constant Contact

- Others

• Content

- Text editor

- Device to record video

- Video editing software

- Device to record audio

- Audio editing software

• Target market

- External storage space
    - Amazon S3
    - Google Drive
    - Vimeo
    - Others
- Back-up plug-in and external space for back-ups
- Squeeze page software or plug-in, or an HTML editor

Picking Membership Software

Now it's time to pick out a membership plug-in. There are dozens of programs out there to help you set up membership areas on your site. I encourage you to do a web search, and a search on WordPress.org, for software that you think will work for your site.

I'm dividing up membership sites into three main types: simple, intermediate and complex. From my own research, I've selected three different plug-ins, one for each level. As of this writing, all were under current development and being supported. I recommend them, but again I urge you to do your own research. A better plug-in might appear between the time I write this and your reading of the book.

Simple

A simple membership site doesn't require software that does a lot of fancy stuff. If you just want to separate non-members from members, and give members a restricted place of their own, you don't need a plug-in that's hard to understand or hard to administer. For that kind of site, I recommend WP-Members, by Rocketgeek Interactive. It can block posts, pages or both. It configures most of its own options, and even warns you if your current WordPress configurations would hinder its proper operation. It sets up its own special pages, like registration and log-in pages. Although installation and set-up are a breeze, the publishers offer a quick start guide, along with a full manual, all on-line at their site. You can provide access once the new member has completed the registration process, or charge for access to the membership area via PayPal if you pay to register the software and download an additional add-on It's simple, basic, and works almost immediately on installation. If you feel like customizing it, the software has lots of hooks and shortcodes for doing just that. Registration is just $47 per year, which will get you priority support, members only forum, access to the code library, and exclusive plug-in extensions.

Intermediate

If you want to set up more than one level on your site – say: Bronze, Silver and Gold levels – you'll want a plug-in that allows you more complex set-up options. I use Paid Memberships Pro on a number of my sites. In addition to multiple levels, it offers an array of payment gateways, a flexible system for pricing and trial memberships, as well as back-end goodies like admin reports, a robust member email system, and SEO (Search Engine Optimization) configuration. Set-up and configuration docs are available on the publisher's site after a no-cost registration. $97 gets you a year's access to premium support, a member's area, and additional add-ons.

Complex

Let's say you've come up with an idea for a site that has multiple levels, multiple post categories, and different types of post contents. And let's say you want to move members up the level ladder automatically. Perhaps you want to offer new registrants several membership options, and want to send them to specific pages once they log in. If you want admin reports on every aspect of your site, with the ability to hide just one word out of an entire post, well then, you want the Wishlist Member plug-in. It's complex, with features and configuration options up the wazoo. Compared to the other plug-ins, it has a steeper learning curve as well. I have it on a few sites, and I'm still not 100% sure I've got it configured correctly; but it will make your membership site do cartwheels. Pricing on this is $97 for one site, or you can install it on an unlimited number of sites for $297.

Personally, I would recommend starting in the middle. Paid Memberships Pro will let you run a simple non-member/member site, but give you the option of creating a more complex system as well. Plus, you get more detailed reporting options. If you need to move up, you can.

Site Design

It's time to start putting together your site! If you're familiar with WordPress, or have followed our link in the back to get some instruction on how to set it up and configure it, then you'll be familiar with the concepts we'll be discussing. If you haven't done either of those, it's not *too* hard to follow along, but I'm not going to guarantee anything. Let's get started.

Themes

WordPress sites are configurable from the ground up. For its outward appearance, WordPress relies on themes. These are file collections that govern the appearance of your site in a visitor's browser. Some themes are very rigid; certain graphics go here, the colors are only such-and-such, you have to use this footer, etc. But many of the new themes allow you to change colors for all sorts of screen elements, like the background or the accent colors. Some allow you to move elements all around the screen. Most allow you to simply drop in an existing logo and have it show up in the header.

There are thousands upon thousands of themes out there. Many are completely free and can be downloaded onto your site from WordPress.org. Within seconds, you can completely change the look of your site. I recommend using themes that are responsive. That is, they can change the position and size of the site's elements based on the type and size of the screen they're being viewed on. The idea is to keep your site readable and interactive on a desktop, a laptop, a tablet or even a smartphone.

There are even more themes out there that you can license. For a fee, you'll get a package including the theme, and perhaps some plug-ins that the authors feel will give you the design experience you want. I have nothing against paying for themes – I've done it a number of times. But I suggest playing with the free themes first. The only thing it'll cost you is time.

Pages

A page is almost like a mini website. You can design a page to hold text, a group of pictures, or put in links you want people to be able to download. Each page can be unique. At the very least, I recommend a Welcome page, where people entering your site can learn a bit about it, and another page – perhaps named Members – where your posts will show up. Obviously, this page would be available only to those who have registered for your site.

A quality site will also have a page where members can control their memberships, where options might include upgrading or renewing their account, changing their password, or opting out completely. You might also have pages that contain information that is different from or more important than the information in your lesson posts.

For all three of the membership plug-ins I've recommended here, the plug-in itself will create new pages and direct people to them at the appropriate times. You may also have the option of creating your own pages, styling them on your own and re-directing people to those instead.

Over the years, I've found that the simpler the site, the better it is for everyone. If people start asking you questions about where to find what, you might have gone overboard with your design.

Menus

Which brings us to menus. This is a system of links that allow people to navigate around your site. You might have a menu across the top of your site, or down one side. You might have a duplicate menu in a footer. Some membership plug-ins allow you to have more than one menu. It might show one set of navigation links to a non-member (or a member who hasn't logged into the site on this visit), and show a different one to people who have successfully logged in. If you have a more complex site with multiple member levels (Bronze, Silver and Gold as an example), you might be able to set up a different menu for each level.

Posts or Lessons

Our next chapter goes in-depth on putting together posts or lessons into Courses.

Categories

Categories are words that WordPress allows you to use to break your content up into major and minor groupings. You can have main categories, and sub-categories. If you have anything other than a very simple member site, I would suggest using them to help segment the content for you and your users. If you have multiple levels or courses (Bronze, Silver, and Gold; Low and High; etc.), I suggest creating overall categories using the same names. If you segment your lessons into sub-categories (Low – wood, Low – plastic, Low – metal), then create these words and apply them to your lessons (posts) as well.

This will allow you to organize your content creation process, and also allow your members to more logically keep track of the lessons they're taking on your site.

Headers, footers & side bars

This is where you'll put the "housekeeping' content of your site, information that everyone needs to see, like menus and links to contact information. You might also put up important announcements here ("Next session starts on August 7th"), as well as make registration/log-in links available here. Widgets (add-ons for WordPress that enhance the site, but don't really change it) often appear in the side bars.

You *do* have your site name and logo in the header, don't you?

Squeeze page

When you place advertisements on other sites to bring them back to your site, you might bring them directly to a squeeze page. This is a page that is designed to either get a visitor's contact information in return for a free download, or get them to register for your site. You place a lot of sales text here, and perhaps a sales video as well. It's usually designed to have several opportunities on the page for the visitor to enter their information as they go down through it, experiencing the sales letter. You might offer them special pricing, or bonus content not available any other way.

There is an art to designing the look and content of a good

squeeze page, and some people pay good money for consultants to help them with this.

Plug-ins & widgets

Plug-ins and widgets operate behind the scenes to change how your WordPress installation functions. They may add features to enhance the operation of your site. For instance, a membership plug-in allows you to control access to your content, restricting it only to people who are registered for your site. It can also help define that content into levels or courses. Widgets often bring useful features to the site, like having a calendar in the side bar, but they don't change how the site functions.

At the end of this book, you'll find a chapter where we list a number of add-ons. Some we deem essential, and others are just nice to have.

Example site set-ups

- Simple:

  - Non-member vs. Member

  - Lessons (posts) – protected or open to everyone

- Intermediate:

  - Different courses or levels

  - Multiple categories and sub-categories

  - Lessons (posts) – open or protected by course (level)

  - Additional pages

  - Different non-member and logged-in member menus

- Complex:

  - All of the above, plus

  - Dripped content

- Content in different languages
- Shopping carts
- Discussion forums
- Almost anything else you can think of

Scott A. Gardner

Creating Lessons & Courses

WordPress, as I mentioned before, was created as a blogging platform. In blogging, you create posts, which are the discrete entries where the content you want to provide your viewers is stored. When you add a membership plug-in to WordPress, it adds additional functionality. In many cases, you can split your members, and the content to which they have access, into levels. You could think of these levels as advancing upwards, like the rungs of a ladder. That's why on many membership sites, you'll find levels that correspond to a hierarchy - Bronze, Silver and Gold; Low and High; Child, Adult and Senior; Private, Captain, Colonel and General, and so forth.

During the course of this book, I've been using different words for these concepts. The individual posts you create to explain one concept I've been calling *lessons*. And while you can refer to groups of people as levels, I've been thinking of groups of lessons, all teaching one main topic, as *courses*. Functionally, there's no difference, so if you want to call it a post instead of a lesson, by all means feel free to do that!

Let's say you create a site, and you want three levels of content. We'll use Bronze, Silver and Gold. Plus, you're going to create some lessons or posts that unregistered visitors can view as well. The first thing we'll do is create four categories. On the Admin page, in the left hand column, go down to Posts, then Categories. The dialogues to create new categories will show up in the center of the page. Let's create the following four:

•Free

•Bronze

•Silver

•Gold

If you enter the names in the Categories box and hit ENTER, the "slug" line will fill in for itself. The slug is how search engines and other 'bots will see the name of the category.

Now go back to the Admin menu, select Posts – Add New. The first thing you'll be asked to enter is the name. Here's my advice: always start any true lesson with the name of the level, plus a number. Since we're putting together our first lesson for Bronze level members, let's name the post "Bronze 01: First Post." If you've configured WordPress to do so, the slug name, as it appears under the Post Name, will be some variation of the subject line and not a random number.

In the body of the post, let's write something like, "This is the first lesson for Bronze level members."

There are a lot of options for a post! Near the top of the right hand column, you'll see an option to publish the post immediately, or to set a date and time for the post. Under that, you'll see checkboxes containing the names of all the categories you just created. There's an option for adding keywords, or tags that might be able to help get your posts found by search engines. If you've installed the All in One SEO plug-in (see the Add-ons chapter), you'll see other options below the body of the post for tweaking the way the post would be shown to search engines.

Depending on the membership plug-in you installed, you'll probably see options for showing this post or lesson to certain membership level members. Since this is a Bronze level post, be sure to check off or select Bronze.

If you want new registrants to go through your levels in order, you might leave it with just Bronze level selected. However, I set sites up to entice visitors to pay for top-level training on signup. If they're already at the top, they will have skipped over Bronze and Silver levels, and gone straight to Gold. If you want them to be able to experience the lower level lessons as well, make sure your selections here allow all levels of members to see the post. As you create higher level lessons, you want to make sure that lower level members don't see the posts. If we were creating a Silver level post here, you would select Silver and Gold levels only. With a Gold level post, you'd want just the highest level to be able to see the lesson, so you'd only select Gold. Many of the membership plug-ins are different, so make sure you read the instructions and understand how to apply this principle in the software you've chosen.

If you have video for your lessons stored off-site, you can embed them right in your post. It's really easy with YouTube and Vimeo videos, especially if you have no other content for the lesson. Find the video you uploaded to their site, and search for the "embed" button. This will give you some code that you can plug directly into your post (lesson), and when a member views the post, they'll see your video waiting to be played.

I suggest using YouTube to post your promotional and free video content. YouTube is browsed by millions of people each week, and you want this type of content to be found. You want to be tripped over by people who didn't even know you existed. Vimeo, in addition to having fewer visitors, allows you to hide content from them. That is, only people who have registered for your course will know your videos exist. There are other options for storing content elsewhere, like Google Cloud and Amazon S3 accounts.

Most people retain more of your information if you use several different types of media. You can include photos, graphics and PDFs as well.

As you create individual Lessons, you want to fit them into a Course. This is a subject that you explain using the lessons and generally follows a progression from introductory content, to more complex or difficult content and ends either on a high point, or with a recap of the Course content.

If you have a lot of content, you might want to break the Courses up into Levels, where a member might go from an introductory course to an intermediate course to a master class.

Example

DressYourselfProperly.info

You work in a men's clothing store, and you get the same questions over and over. What should I wear, and how do I put it all on? You've even had a couple side commissions being the "personal dresser" for upwardly mobile business executives. Given your position, you know there are a lot of guys out there who could use help. Not just the advanced topics, but even the most foundational features of getting dressed seem to be beyond some men. Perhaps they're afraid to ask. Maybe they want to learn in the comfort and privacy of their own home.

You've heard about membership web sites before. *Hey, you think, maybe I can help them out and keep earning money on the side.*

First, you need a site name that fits in with the site you want to run. You visit GoDaddy.com and register the site name DressYourselfProperly.info. Next, you'll need the space to run it. You sign up for a site at OnyxBusinessHosting.com and ask for the WordPress-based site package to be installed.

That was the easy part. Now it's time to start thinking about your content. You start listing lesson topics on a sheet of paper.

• Slipping into a tuxedo jacket

• Putting on your socks

• Tying a half Windsor

• Tying your shoes

• Putting on underwear

You realize that putting these into a logical order would be helpful. You also realize, while completing your lesson list, that you could build three whole courses from your lessons: Casual, Business and Formal.

You know that you want to get paid for this instruction, so you're going to have to choose a payment processor. But you want to create some basic content that you can give away for free as a way of enticing people to join your site. You realize that the three courses could be multiple levels on the same site, offered in different ways. Obviously, the simplest membership software isn't going to work here. You need something that will handle payments and multiple levels, so you choose the Intermediate software.

You complete your list of lessons, separating them into three courses, or levels. You also realize that each course talks about three layers of clothing. You create a series of main and sub-categories for your posts, just to keep things neat and tidy.

•Casual

- Casual – underclothes
- Casual – main
- Casual – outerwear

•Business

- Business – underclothes
- Business – main
- Business – outerwear

•Formal

- Formal – underclothes
- Formal – main
- Formal – outerwear

You've created a simple structure for your site, your courses, and your course content. Now you need to start creating the content and setting up the pages and posts to make it available. You know that to keep the interest and attention of people, you should have a mix of media that makes up your content. You decide to make some illustrated articles available for download, along with some video demonstrations about how to size, put on, and wear some of the clothing items.

As you're working on the content, you decide that shooting three different sock videos is unnecessary. But, should you use just one post in Casual and reference it in all three courses? That may not work, and you decide some members might be confused. So you take the lesson text and the link to the sock video, and duplicate it into new posts for the Business and Formal lessons.

During your breaks from creating lesson content, you build other pages to go on the site. First you create a Welcome page. You write some introductory text, and you plan on putting a short video on there as well. You also create a Links page, to give visitors access to other important articles and videos. You write down that you want to create a Member Account page, but you'll wait until after you install the membership plug-in.

You also search WordPress.org for a clean, simple theme. You try about half a dozen before you settle on one that allows you to set the colors you want, and insert the snazzy new logo your friend designed for you. The theme also uses responsive design, and even looks good on your smart phone.

Now it's time to install the membership plug-in. You choose Paid Memberships Pro and set up the three levels (courses) you created lessons for. You decide to enable taking payments via Stripe.com so that you get your money fairly quickly. You enable it and put it into test mode.

As you're finishing up your content creating, it's time to start testing out how the site's going to work. First, you open a different browser program and visit your page. You register for the site at the Casual level, verify your email address and log in. Everything's empty, but seems to be functioning fine. You go back to your site set-up, and add two more members; one at Business level, and another at Formal level. You'll use each of these three member log-ins to check out your site several times during completion, and after going live.

Once you've got your lesson (post) text written, your video

edited, stored somewhere and linked in, and all your PDFs stored and linked to, it's time to ask for some help. You turn to a few friends and ask them to please register for the site and try to break it. Ask them to contact you with any errors in the content, any links that don't work, and so forth. It's essential that you ask them to do all sorts of things you never designed the site to do in the first place. This is the best way to find out what doesn't work like you intended it to. You don't want real paying customers complaining that Lesson #4 is missing, or that the link to your sock video is showing how to put on galoshes.

Planning ahead, you want to make sure you put yourself in front of your target audience – fashion conscious upwardly mobile male executives. You know a blogger who writes about fashion for a national audience, so you reach out to him and invite him and a few of his friends to try your membership site at no charge, with the idea that he'll write about it. You also know that there are several trade shows scheduled over the summer in the city where you live. You decide to investigate getting a booth at one of them, or possibly sharing a booth with someone else. Finally, you take some of your lessons and re-write them into short articles. You send some of these to fashion blogs and magazines, and others you upload to eZineArticles.com with the idea of generating some links back to your member site.

Now you make the corrections your friends have suggested, and make the credit card processor live. You visit your site again, this time pulling out a credit card to register for your site. Everything goes smoothly.

It's now time to announce your new membership site to the world!

Action Items

1) Write down content topics and lessons you might want to offer. The best subject matter is probably something you're very familiar with. This could be related to your job, or it might be a hobby or other pastime you enjoy and know a lot about.

2) Define your target market. Who would need the content you want to teach? What types of media do they consume? Where do they work? What types of recreation do they enjoy? Write out a detailed description of the people you're after, and where you might put yourself in front of them.

3) Once you decide on what you're going to teach your members, try to think of a name for your site that reflects its purpose. It should be something fairly short and to the point. Visit your registrar's web site and use their tools to do a search. If your site name is taken, it may suggest something similar that is available.

4) Do you want to charge for access, or simply collect contact information? This can help you decide what membership plug-in to use, and whether or not to use a payment processor.

5) Will you create some or all of the content? Or will you have to find others who can craft the lessons and courses you want to offer? Start creating or collecting the content.

6) Register your site, find a host, and install WordPress. Install the basic plug-ins you'll need to work behind the scenes, and start trying out different themes. Start with free themes first, and then, if you have to, start looking at paid themes.

7) Start breaking your content down into an orderly progression. Define courses (if needed), lessons, and categories. Multiple types of media are best, so line up video, audio and graphics-based content, and any help you might need to produce and edit them for presentation.

8) Investigate membership plug-ins and then install the one that best fits how you want to administer your site.

9) Start turning some of your content into pieces you can offer

to blogs, magazines, and other media. Consider offering pieces to media that aren't directly matched with your content, but are complimentary to it (fashion articles to a business blog, or technology tips to a travel magazine).

10) Find friends and colleagues to help you test your site, and the content delivery. Make changes and corrections, and do it again.

11) Go live. Announce your site on-line on social media sites (Facebook, Twitter, LinkedIn, etc.) and in media sites related to your content (trade magazines, related blogs, etc.). Start putting yourself in front of your target market.

Final Words

We've come to the end of the book, but this is only the beginning of your journey. I've used the exact same techniques I've described here to set up membership sites for my clients, and for some of my own projects.

But remember, a membership site of any kind is just an electronic collection of your content without members to consume it. To get someone interested in using your site, you must get it in front of your target market. And to get their interest, you will want to have some quality information to give them that will paint you as an expert in their eyes. If you're going to pay to learn information, you want to learn from the best!

Right now, though, I hope you're fired up. I want you to be excited about putting together a membership site. You can do it! I urge you to go back through the book, and highlight important passages. If you've got the print book, feel free to mark it up. If you're reading a digital copy, make notes on paper or in a text file. Refer back to the book as you put your own site together.

As I said earlier, this book concentrates on creating membership sites that help teach your concepts or information. But there are membership sites out there that do other things. Using some of the basic tenets presented here, you can build those as well. Use your imagination and let it run wild.

If you have questions, please feel free to visit the companion site for the book. We'll have an FAQ section, and other venues for exchanging information.

www.MembershipSiteMoney.com

I look forward to hearing about your success!

Installing Themes & Plug-ins

There are thousands upon thousands of themes and plug-ins available for WordPress. Many are available totally for free, others on the freemium distribution model, where the original is provided at no cost, while the same theme or plug-in with additional features is available for a fee. Some are only available on paying a licensing or registration fee.

I strongly suggest that you start by exploring the add-ons available through WordPress.org. Many of those can be installed at no cost. You can play with an add-on and see if it meets your requirements. Then, if you decide to pay (if the publisher even charges for an upgrade) you can. If it doesn't work like you want it to, or if you have problems administering it, there are probably at least half a dozen other add-ons in the same category that you can try instead.

The mechanics of searching and installing are fairly easy. First, log into your WordPress site as the Administrator. If you want a new theme, select Appearance/Themes from the left side menu. Looking for a new plug-in? Go to Plugins/Add New.

Themes

For a new theme, you want to select the Add New button at the top. WordPress will begin by giving you tabs to look at their current Featured, Popular and Latest themes. There's also a Search Themes dialog box over on the right. This is great if you know the name – or part of the name – of a particular theme you've seen or heard of.

A Feature Filter button brings up a list of settings, where you can filter their entire inventory of themes based on different layout and feature configurations. I might argue that the Color filter is no longer valid, as most themes now allow you to specify colors after set-up. Most of the time you'll hit on older themes, but if you have a specific color you want to stick with, you might try these as well.

Once WordPress gives you a visual list of the themed that meet your search criteria, hover your mouse over one. You'll see a button for Details & Preview. If you click here, you'll find out what the theme's publisher has to say. Another window will pop up on your screen, giving you a demo of the basic look of the theme on your right, and info on the left. If you want to install it, click the Install button at the top of the left hand window. If not, click Close and keep looking!

Once you install a new theme, you need to Activate it if you want others to see it on your site. You can also get a Live Preview to allow you to see what it will look like on your site, without having to activate it.

Plug-ins

To start looking for a new plug-in, you can enter your desired phrase, description or name in the dialog box. Below, there is a tag cloud of the most popular search terms. If one of those matches what you're looking for, just click on it.

WordPress returns a list of plug-ins that match the phrase you entered. On the left is a list of the plug-ins, with their descriptions on the right. Under the plug-in's name are usually two links. One will automatically install the plug-in, while the other takes you to a page giving you more details. I recommend giving the Details link a look before you install the plug-in. One of the important pieces of info provided is the length of time it's been since the publisher upgraded the software. If it's been over 6 months, you might want to reconsider installing it. If the publisher isn't updating it, will they continue to support it going forward?

And that's how easy it is to install new themes or plug-ins for your membership site!

Add-ons

Membership plug-ins -

•WP-MEMBERS – www.RocketGeek.com

•Paid Memberships Pro – www.PaidMembershipsPro.com

•Wishlist Member – www.WishlistMember.com

Strongly suggested plug-ins -

•Akismet

•SEO All-In-One

•UpdraftPlus backup

Totally optional -

•Simple Custom Post Order

•WPBadger

•Events Calendar

•WP Lead Plus squeeze page creator

•Simple:Press forum

Definitions

Administrator (Admin): Person with responsibility for running a WordPress site behind the scenes. May include posting content, approving or deleting comments and member account management. Could be the person who designed the site, or someone the owner or designer has appointed.

Course: A collection of lessons (posts) covering a particular topic. Might be separated by category, membership level, or both.

Forum: A specialized plug-in or piece of software designed to facilitate open discussion among users and possibly administrators. Can be a single forum with multiple topics, or multiple forums with one or more topics each.

Lesson: A post made by an administrator that covers one specific learning objective. May contain text, video, audio and other viewable or downloadable files.

Level: Some membership plug-ins allow the designer to set up multiple groups (I.e. Bronze, Silver and Gold). Groups of lessons designed to be viewed by members of a level are called Courses.

Member: A person who has completed the designer's proscribed enrollment process, and has been allowed access to some or all of the secured content of a membership site.

Plug-in: A piece of software added on to WordPress that changes the installation's features or functionality.

Post: A blog entry created by the owner, designer or an administrator, usually as a Lesson for members. Depending on the design of the site, members may be able to respond to the information in a post by attaching a comment to it.

Payment Processor: A company that takes a credit card payment for something (membership access, a downloadable file, a physical product to be shipped, etc.), deducts a handling fee, and then turns over the rest of the payment to the site owner.

Target Market: A group of individuals who possess the social, economic and demographic qualities desired to make them customers of a company or individual. Regardless of their individual dynamics, each person should have a particular want or need that is answered by the marketer's product or service.

Theme: A file or group of files capable of being installed into a WordPress site that alters the way the site looks on – and possibly interacts with – a visitor's web browser.

Links

Registrars

- GoDaddy

- NameCheap

- PowerPipe

Web hosts

- Onyx Business Hosting

- Hawk Host

Off-site storage

- Amazon S3

- Google Cloud

- Vimeo

Learning WordPress

- WordPress 101 – Installing WordPress

- WordPress Beginner

Other Links

- Moodle – www.Moodle.org

Scott A. Gardner

Registering your book

I want to sincerely thank you for purchasing my book explaining *Membership Site Design.* If you found it useful, I'd ask that you do a couple things.

First, please register your copy at this address -

http://membershipsitemoney.com/book-registration/

This will add you to a mailing list I keep **ONLY** for informing my readers about new books, or about major revisions to books I've published. You'll get a welcome email, and then emails only when I put out a new book.

Second, please take a moment to leave a review on-line. I hope if you found the book useful you'll leave a 4- or 5-star review.

Now, get to work on those Action Items and start building your membership site today!

Excerpt – Recognized Expert Status

For more information, visit http://amzn.to/1r6q3Vm

Definition

People complain to one another. A lot. And in our society, when they do, the people listening often offer up solutions. They mention the people they know or have heard of who can help alleviate the pain. That's very general, so let's give some better examples.

> *Adam and Bob are talking over a couple beers in Adam's basement. Adam points to a dark spot on the ceiling.*
>
> *"I've got a leak somewhere up there, and it's ruining my ceiling. I've gotta get that fixed."*
>
> *"That sucks," says Bob. "I had the same problem a while back. Wally from Wally's Plumbing came over and fixed me up. It took a couple days, but it hasn't leaked since. I'll email you his contact info when I get home."*

Here's another.

> *Larry and Vanessa are in a meeting, discussing solutions for some of the problems their company is facing.*
>
> *"We need to find out why those bearings in the new wheels are giving out so quickly. We need to find an engineering company that can study them and help us find an answer," says Larry.*
>
> *"I found a video on line," says Vanessa. "This guy is explaining his company's testing procedures. It looks pretty good. You should watch it."*

And one more.

> *Lucy pours Joyce a cup of coffee and then sits*

down at the kitchen table.

*"I'm running out of room around here. My food
storage containers are spilling out of every
cupboard," says Lucy, "and the ones I have in
the fridge are taking up way too much room."*

*"You're in luck," says Joyce. "Suzie across the
street is a RubberWare rep, and she's got some
great products that take up almost no space.
She's got a RubberWare party coming up next
week. We should go and pick up a few things."*

*"Sounds great," says Lucy. "You know, you
almost sound like a commercial for Suzie!"*

How do we find products and services? Sure, we have a bunch
of search services literally at our fingertips. There's the Internet,
and we still have the Yellow Pages, even if they are a shade of
what they used to be. There are trade and service organizations
that can help you select one of their members, and if you're
looking for something in a strange city, your hotel might have a
concierge.

But many times, we simply take the word of someone else,
friend or stranger. If they point us toward someone, we often
follow their advice. Personal recommendations are the strongest
means for delivering new business to a company.
Overwhelmingly, we like to recommend the people who
specialize in fixing the kinds of problems our friends are
experiencing. If someone wants to add a deck to their house, we
don't want to recommend someone who builds garages, we want
to recommend someone who is an expert at building decks.

As a friend, we want to recommend experts to others. As a
business person, we want to be the expert who gets
recommended to others. We want to be that Recognized Expert.

A Recognized Expert is someone whom others believe to be the
best in their industry or niche. They are known for their depth of
knowledge on a particular subject. As the face of their business,
they are known to provide superior products or services. They
might have certifications and awards that provide proof of their

expertise. Certainly they have people from their past successes who can testify to their prowess in their specialization.

A Recognized Expert can only be a person. You cannot create a fictional character for your business and "give" it RecEx Status. So developing RecEx Status is not for everyone. If you are timid, reclusive, and hate having your name in the media, you may not be the ideal RecEx for your business.

RecEx Status is very similar to other types of celebrity status, but instead of being known to the general public, a RecEx specializes in promoting their status within their industry or niche, and among their clients and potential clients. During a speech he was giving, I once heard a RecEx describe himself as "the most famous person people outside of this room have never heard of." That specialized celebrity is not cultivated just for the sake of free drinks or being asked for autographs. A RecEx uses her status to more easily reach their target market, and to earn greater profit from their work.

Many, many people have expertise in their field. Their knowledge may be unmatched by their competitors, the quality of their work unassailable. Many experts are not the head of the companies they work for, and they don't necessarily want to be the owner or CEO of a business. And that's just fine! At one time, I was a computer tech at a mid-sized environmental engineering firm. My "target market" was the 250 or so employees in the building where I worked. My focus was on convincing them that I was more knowledgeable about their computers and the computer problems they experienced than my "competitor," the other computer tech within the company. I didn't care if anyone outside the company knew who I was.

The problem isn't necessarily "expertise," but the failure to be recognized for it by your competitors and your target market. Very much like the tree falling in a forest, if you have expertise and no one knows it, are you really an expert?

Benefits

The object of becoming recognized for your expertise is to extend the reach and power of your existing marketing efforts. The trappings of a properly implemented RecEx Status can help tip a buying decision in your favor, and reduce buyer remorse after the transaction.

Unless you are the only person in your geographic region who does your particular job, then you have competition. Imagine what a potential consumer of your product or service goes through to choose a supplier.

- Define exactly what they want

- Find a list of as many suppliers as possible

- Decide the differences between suppliers

- Attempt to discern the quality of the suppliers' products and services

- Ask for pricing and delivery

- Make a final decision on whom to go with

A properly crafted RecEx Status makes the job easier for the prospective client. It can help them know right up front that you're not the person for them. And that's actually a plus for you, as your status helps potential customers self-qualify themselves, and those who choose not to include you in their decision process leave you more time to spend on true prospects.

The first problem prospects face is compiling a list of all possible people who might be able to provide a solution to their problem. Some businesses never get clients because the prospect pool never even finds out they exist. Not only do you want to make it onto a prospect's radar, you want to be at the top of the list. A RecEx can make it there.

Next, a prospect tries to figure out the major differences between possible suppliers. Whether they call it that or not, the prospect is trying to choose a position for each name on that list. Imagine a box broken up into four quadrants. The vertical line in the center of the box is graduated from one extreme of a factor at the bottom, to the extreme opposite at the top. The horizontal axis is graduated from one extreme at the left to the opposite on the right. These factors are usually complimentary. The stereotypical positioning axes have "quality" as the vertical scale (low at the bottom to high at the top), and "price" as the horizontal axis (low at the left, high right). This is called a position map.

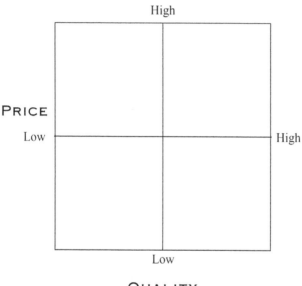

You want to use your Expert Proof Materials (EPM – more on those later), along with your other marketing tactics, to carve out a space on your prospect's position map where you have few or no direct competition. If you have no competition, and you're promoting the product or service the prospect is looking for, then you're probably going to get a call.

With competition, the prospect will have to consider other factors. Let's be blunt – all things being equal, they're probably going to flip a coin, or choose a popular name, or pick the closest company to solve their problem.

What you do not want is "all things being equal." You want to disrupt the playing field, put yourself on your own mountain towering over all your non-competitors. Ideally, you want to be introduced to the prospect by one of their friends as the best solution – the only solution – for their needs.

In the good old days of mass media, if it ever actually worked, the idea was that if a prospect saw a particular ad enough times, they would trot along dutifully and purchase whatever you were selling. The marketer was trying to compel members of the public to buy a particular whatsit.

But the Holy Grail of marketing is the prospect's peer who, without being paid, recommends the marketer's product or service. When that happens, sales statistics go through the roof.

While your EPM and other marketing efforts will reaffirm your prospect's decision, it's being recommended as the expert that will make the sale. As a RecEx, you'll have dozens – perhaps hundreds or thousands – of unpaid salespeople running around and promoting you. Think of how much it costs to hire even one part-time sales person!

Once you've been recommended, you can present your EPM and other marketing materials. Unless the prospect is searching based solely on price (and no matter what you hear from other sales people and business owners, most aren't!), you have the opportunity to actually quote the prospect a higher price, and still make a sale.

Happy customers become happy non-paid salespeople, recommending you to others and thereby driving your sales numbers even higher. You have more people out and about selling for you, all the while earning higher profits.

And finally, with the combination of your EPM and your RecEx Status, you'll find yourself dealing with fewer sales prospects, people who need to be convinced to buy your product or service. You'll notice you're doing more "order taking" than "sales making" as your materials and RecEx Status do the selling for you.

With a carefully crafted and implemented RecEx Status, benefits include -

- Lower cost per sale
- Higher profits
- More sales coverage
- Pre-made sales

Doesn't this sound like something that's worth developing?

■ ■

To purchase *Recognized Expert Status*, please visit

http://amzn.to/1r6q3Vm

Acknowledgments

I want to thank my proofreaders *par excellence*, Ken Darrow and Angela Matias. Any mistakes left here are purely my own. I can recommend them wholeheartedly.

You can visit Angela's LinkedIn account here:

https://www.linkedin.com/pub/angela-matias/16/361/585

Ken has an editing gig on Fiverr.com. You can find his profile here:

http://www.fiverr.com/mrproofreader